JUNETEENTH

A Children's Story

written by
Opal LEE

illustrated by Peter Viska

*This book is dedicated to all the children of the United States
that need to be made aware of their history.
Please be sure to tell them about the 13th, 14th and 15th Amendments
to the Constitution when they are older.*

ACKNOWLEDGMENTS

To my Savior the Lord Jesus Christ for affording me these 94 years.

My grandparents, the Rev. Z. and Mattie Broadous, for the zeal and zest that they passed on to me.

My mother, Mattie Bell Broadous Flake, who believed in me regardless of the many mistakes and missteps I made.

The late Rev. Ronald Meyers, Sr., MD, founder of the National Juneteenth Observance Foundation for asking me to serve on the Board of a cause I truly believe in.

Tanya Starks for insisting and insisting and insisting that I write this book for children.

My granddaughter, Dione Sims, whose faithfulness in the many projects we've undertaken is unheralded.

The children asked, "Grand Dear Opal Lee, what does this say?"
"Juneteenth, a Children's Story, that's the title of the book," she replied.
"Grand Dear, can you please read this book to us?"

Over 200 years ago, people who looked like me were slaves.

Someone may have read to you the stories
from the Bible about slaves in Egypt,
but they were not like these slaves.

Men from this country and other countries stole people in Africa from their fathers, mothers, brothers, and sisters.

They chained them up and brought them across the ocean in ships.

That's a lot of water and a very long trip.
Some did not make it.

The enslaved Africans
were forced to work
very hard for no
pay and were not treated fairly.
Life was not good for them.

There was a US President, like President Barack Obama, named Abraham Lincoln who declared slaves would be free on January 1, 1863. This was called the Emancipation Proclamation.

By the President of the United States of America:

A Proclamation.

Whereas, on the twenty-second day of
September ... our Lord one thousand
... ...

"... shall then be in rebellion against ...

"United States, shall be then, thenceforward, and

"forever free; and the Executive Government of th...

"United States, including the military ...

"... whereof shall then be in rebellion against the

"United States, shall be then, thenceforward, and

"forever free; and the Executive Government of th...

"... thereof, will recognize and maintain

"... persons, and will do no act ...

"... or any of them,

The enslaved waited at churches all night long on New Year's Eve to see how freedom would come. These were called "Watch Night" services, and many churches still hold them today.

The United States was so big that Texas did not get enforcement of the Emancipation Proclamation for two-and-a-half years after slavery had ended.

US Colored Troops and Major General Gordon Granger arrived in Galveston, Texas and on June 19, 1865 read General Order No. 3 to the people that were there.

Then he nailed it to the door of what
is now Reedy Chapel AME Church.
General Granger declared,

ALL SLAVES ARE FREE!

The slaves were so happy that they started celebrating and we've been celebrating, ever since!

Every year since, there have been celebrations and the formerly enslaved put on their best clothes, "dressed to the nines", to celebrate their freedom!

This day was called "Juneteenth" and is celebrated in the United States and around the World.

Each year on the 19th of June, people celebrate the ending of slavery with festivals, concerts, and educational activities.

Teacher's Guide and Parent Notes

While our book focuses on the historical facts surrounding the freedom of the enslaved in the State of Texas, it is very important to understand why celebrating Juneteenth all across the country is important. This guide of facts is available to provide you with resources to best explain the significance of the holiday recognition.

Isn't Juneteenth just about Texas?

While the celebration of June 19th or Juneteenth originated in Texas because it was a day when actual enslaved people were freed through the enforcement of the Emancipation Proclamation in the State of Texas, celebrating is in no way limited to Texas. There were several people from all over the nation involved with delivering the news of freedom to the enslaved in Texas. For example, the US Colored Troops (USCT) were units from Illinois and New York. General Gordon Granger was from New York as well.

Why should June 19th be a National Holiday?

Commemorating important dates on the national calendar is a hallmark of our democracy, therefore the idea of celebrating the abolition of slavery is a cause worth honoring with a holiday. There are a number of significant occurrences on or around the 19th of June that reinforce the selection of June 19th or Juneteenth as the right day to commemorate the original civil liberty of freedom. The events listed can be further researched as supporting facts to the national holiday discussion:

June 19, 1862   Slavery outlawed in US territories by Congress with President Lincoln signing and approving the Chapter CXI – **An Act to secure Freedom for all Persons within the Territories of the United States**

June 19, 1863	Pennsylvania Abolitionist Society enforce the Emancipation order
June 19, 1863	Orders to authorize the formation of the USCT
June 19, 1865	USCT 29 & 31 and General Gordon Granger deliver General Order #3 in Galveston, TX
June 14, 1866	Four treaties signed with the Five Civilized Tribes - Cherokee, Creek, Seminole and combined Chickasaw and Choctaw - ends slavery in Oklahoma Territory
June 19, 1964	Civil Rights Act of 1964 survived an 83-day filibuster in the Senate.
June 19, 1968	Poor People's Campaign Solidarity Day March, Washington D.C.

Does it matter what day freedom is celebrated on?

While freedom for the enslaved came on different days in each state or territory, requesting a national day to celebrate as a whole country seeks to build unity and bring education and enlightenment through commemorating the ability to enjoy FREEDOM for all. Not every state acknowledges the abolition of slavery on the anniversary of when it occurred for them, but 47 of the 50 states do have a Day of Observance for Juneteenth on their records.

Like celebrating Christmas on December 25th of every year, the National Juneteenth Observance Foundation (NJOF) seeks for legislation to ensure that Freedom for the enslaved will always be commemorated and the truth about the triumphs and the tragedies can be taught openly without fear or shame.

Other People to Study

William Lloyd Garrison

John Brown

Sojourner Truth

Frederick Douglass

Nat Turner

Rev. Ronald Myers, Sr., MD

Private William Costley

Harriet Tubman

QUOTES

"Unity is strength...when there is teamwork and collaboration, wonderful things can be achieved."
- Mattie Stepanek

"The whole world opened to me when I learned to read."
- Mary McLeod Bethune

"What makes America great is freedom, but we've got a hundred more rows to hoe." - The Sankoffer

"Learn to do common things uncommonly well; we must always keep in mind that anything that helps fill the dinner pail is valuable."
- George Washington Carver

ISBN: 978 1 51368 491 8 (HB)
ISBN 978 1 51368 490 1 (PB)

Copyright © 2019 by Opal Lee
Illustrations copyright © Peter Viska 2021
Cover and text designed by Sandra Nobes

Registration Number: TXu002144859 / 2019-04-18 Unity Unlimited Inc.
2119 Harrison Avenue
Fort Worth, TX, 76110-1105

CPSIA information can be obtained
at www.ICGtesting.com
Printed in the USA
BVHW021653070621
608955BV00006B/116